SPOOKY SKATERS

THE SKATE PARK AFTER DARK

ANGELA SALT & STUART HARRISON

STARTER LEVEL

SCHOLASTIC

Material written by: Angela Salt
Illustrator: Stuart Harrison
Publisher: Jacquie Bloese
Editor: Patricia Reilly
Designer: Mo Choy
Picture research: Emma Bree
Photo credits:
Pages 26 & 27: Tristar/Everett/Rex; J. Tree,
D. MacDonald/Alamy; G. Reda/Corbis; J. Toreno/Riser,
J. McDonald/Getty Images. **Pages 28 & 29:** B. Molyneux,
P. Bramhill, J. Selby, Danwer Productions/Alamy; S. Kozak,
A. Tanaka/Corbis; R. Levine/Imagebank/Getty images.

Published by Scholastic Ltd. 2007

Mary Glasgow Magazines (Scholastic Ltd.)
Euston House
24 Eversholt Street
London
NW1 1DB

Printed in Brazil

Reprinted in 2008, 2009, 2011, 2014, 2015 and 2016

Impressão e Acabamento: Brasilform Editora e Ind. Gráfica
Lote: 278380

CONTENTS

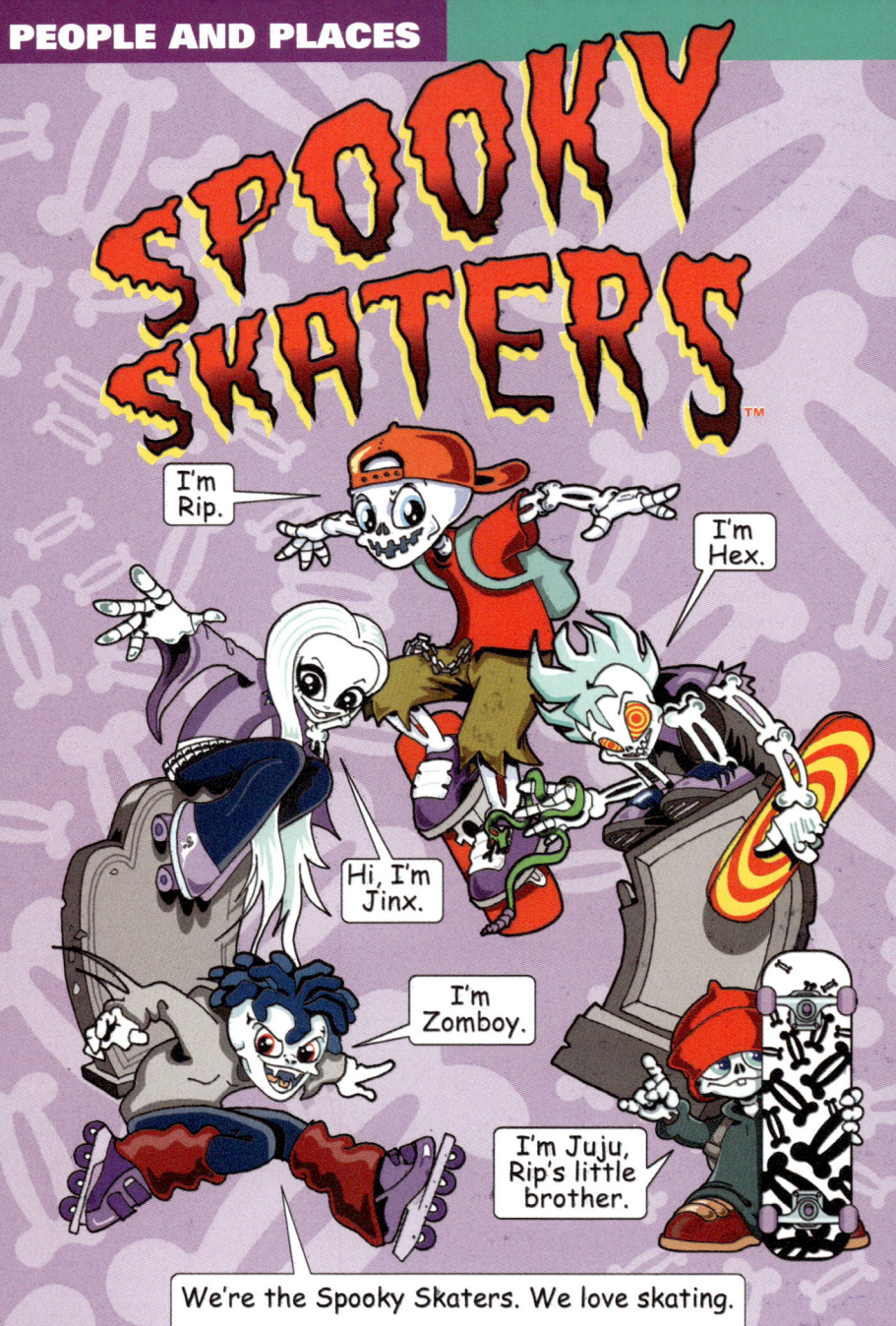

And this is ...

... Patty and Roland. They're brother and sister. They aren't happy because they don't have any friends. They like going to the skate park. Roland's got a new skateboard – but he can't skate.

... Roland and Patty's mum and dad. Their dad has a lot of burger bars. He loves his burger bars – and his money ...

.... Ben and Leila. They love skateboarding. They can do great stunts and they're cool.

PLACES
The skate park: a great place for skating. Ben and Leila and their friends go there every day. Roland and Patty go there too.

SPOOKY SKATERS

THE SKATE PARK AFTER DARK

It's Thursday afternoon at the skate park. Ben, Leila and their friends come here every day after school.

HEY, BEN – WHAT ARE YOU BUILDING?

IT'S A NEW RAMP.

COOL!

Ben works on the ramp all day. Two teenagers watch him for hours …

HEY, FAT BOY! WHAT ARE YOU DOING?!

NOT COOL!

SLIP!

THUD!

HA! HA! HA! HA! HA! HA! HA! HA!

BE QUIET. IT'S NOT FUNNY!

DON'T LAUGH AT MY BROTHER!

It's twelve o'clock at night. Five friends - Rip, Jinx, Zomboy, Hex and Juju - are meeting in a dark, secret place. The Land of the Dead is down under the skate park.

SHH! LISTEN! THE SKATE PARK IS QUIET NOW ...

DEAD QUIET?

YEAH. ARE YOU READY?

YEAH. IT'S TIME TO PLAY!

OPEN THE DOOR, RIP.

CREAKK!

ARE THEY HERE?

DON'T BE STUPID, JINX! IT'S DARK. IT'S LATE.

COME WITH ME, SPOOKY FRIENDS. HERE WE FEEL **ALIVE**!

YEAH. THE LAND OF THE DEAD IS **DEAD** BORING!

BUT THAT'S OUR SECRET, JUJU.

COOL. NO MORE LAND OF THE DEAD.

THIS PLACE IS COOL. I NEVER WANT TO LEAVE.

I KNOW. YOU'RE RIGHT, RIP ...

BUT WE CAN SKATE HERE EVERY NIGHT. COME ON!

BUT WE CAN'T SKATE HERE IN THE DAY. WE'RE NOT FROM HERE - YOU KNOW THAT.

Zomboy and Hex both like Jinx.

IT'S TIME TO DO SOME STUNTS. WATCH THIS, JINX.

NO, WATCH ME. I'M A GREAT SKATER!

WAIT, BOYS. LOOK AT THIS! IT'S A NEW RAMP ...

NOW I'M HAPPY!!

RIP! TEACH ME A COOL STUNT.

OK. YOU CAN LEARN TO DO THIS - A RIP FLIP! SEE?

The Spooky Skaters are having lots of fun at the skate park. They all love the new ramp. Suddenly ...

It's Roland and Patty and their mum and dad!

IT'S DARK, DARLING ... I CAN'T SEE A THING. IT'S SPOOKY ...

LOOK! WHAT DO YOU THINK?

WHAT ARE WE LOOKING AT?!

I HAVE FIFTY BURGER BARS ALL OVER THE COUNTRY. I WANT TO BUILD A NEW BURGER BAR HERE.

BUT THIS IS THE SKATE PARK!

THAT'S RIGHT – AND I'M BUYING IT. NO MORE SKATING! AND LOTS OF MONEY FOR ME ...

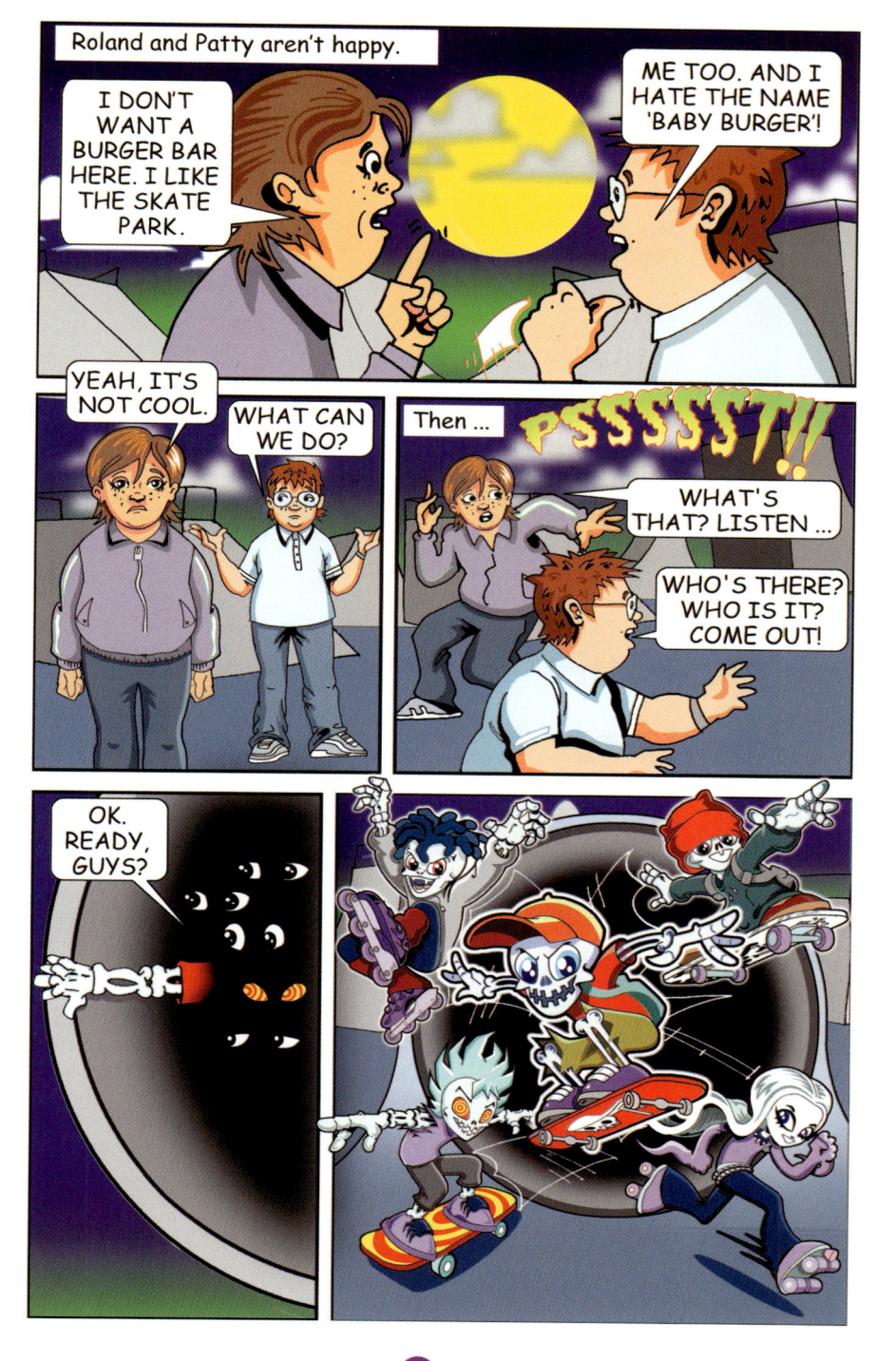

Roland and Patty aren't happy.

I DON'T WANT A BURGER BAR HERE. I LIKE THE SKATE PARK.

ME TOO. AND I HATE THE NAME 'BABY BURGER'!

YEAH, IT'S NOT COOL.

WHAT CAN WE DO?

Then ...

PSSSSST!!

WHAT'S THAT? LISTEN ...

WHO'S THERE? WHO IS IT? COME OUT!

OK. READY, GUYS?

WH-WHO ARE YOU?

G-G-G-G-GO AWAY!

WAIT! DON'T RUN! LISTEN TO US FIRST.

WE'RE THE SPOOKY SKATERS- I'M RIP AND THESE ARE MY FRIENDS.

JINX.

ZOMBOY

HEX

AND I'M JUJU, RIP'S LITTLE BROTHER. REMEMBER THIS FACE!

HEY, WE WANT TO HELP ...

H-H-HOW?

WE LIKE THE SKATE PARK, TOO. IT'S OUR FAVOURITE PLACE. WE COME HERE EVERY NIGHT.

I'M PATTY AND THIS IS MY BROTHER, ROLAND.

WE COME HERE EVERY DAY, BUT WE CAN'T SKATE. WE CAN ONLY WATCH.

AND NOW OUR DAD WANTS TO BUILD A BURGER BAR HERE.

THAT'S TERRIBLE.

YEAH - NO SKATING IS DEAD BORING!

WHEN WE SKATE, WE FEEL ALIVE.

YEAH - NOT DEAD!!

I EAT LOTS OF DAD'S BURGERS. I NEVER FEEL GREAT.

ME TOO. I'M ALWAYS TIRED.

TRUE - YOU TWO HAVE VERY WHITE FACES ...

BUT THEN, YOU ARE SEEING GHOSTS!

WOOOWAAAWOO!

WELL, GUYS, MAYBE WE CAN HELP. YOU WANT TO SKATE? WATCH AND LEARN!

OK, I'M WATCHING. START THE SKATING LESSON.

Roland and Patty are learning to skate.

START WITH THIS

IT'S DIFFICULT, BUT I CAN TRY AGAIN AND AGAIN.

VERY GOOD. HEY, WE'RE THE SPOOKY SKATER TEACHERS!!

WATCH THIS! IT'S MY NEW STUNT - A RIP FLIP!

YOU LEARN FAST, ROLAND - AND YOU TOO, PATTY.

YEAH, THIS IS EXCITING. IT'S FUN!

OH, LOOK! IT'S THREE O'CLOCK, PATTY. WE HAVE SCHOOL TOMORROW. LET'S GO.

YOU CAN LEARN SOME MORE STUNTS TOMORROW NIGHT.

GREAT. SEE YOU AT TWELVE!

Back at Roland and Patty's house ...

THEY'RE NOT IN THEIR ROOMS AGAIN. WHERE ARE THEY? WHERE DO THEY GO EVERY NIGHT?

I'VE GOT AN IDEA.

Next day, at the skate park ...

HEY, DO YOU KNOW THESE TWO?

HEY, LOOK GUYS, IT'S FAT BOY AND HIS SISTER!!

THEY'RE NOT OUR FRIENDS!

YOU'RE IN THE WRONG PLACE - TRY THE BURGER BAR!

HA HA HA!

The next night ...

WOW! YOUR SISTER LOOKS VERY DIFFERENT NOW ... AND WATCH HER SKATE!

YEAH! BUT WHAT CAN I DO TO BE 'STREET' COOL?

HMM ... WHAT ABOUT YOUR HAIR?

A NEW COLOUR IS EASY. WATCH THIS.

THAT'S TERRIBLE!

YEAH, JUJU. THAT'S BAD.

COOL!

GREAT HAIR! DON'T WASH IT!

BUT LOOK! YOUR HAIR'S GREEN NOW.

SKATING HERE WITH YOU EVERY NIGHT IS COOL, BUT...

WE WANT TO TALK TO DAD ABOUT HIS BURGER BAR. WE THINK WE CAN STOP HIM NOW.

THAT'S GREAT!

BYE, GUYS. ALWAYS REMEMBER YOUR SPOOKY SKATER TEACHERS!

YOUR **SECRET** SPOOKY SKATER TEACHERS!!

THANKS. YOU'RE DEAD GOOD FRIENDS!

Patty sends her mum a text.

@sk8 park

DARLING, OUR LITTLE BABY BURGERS ARE AT THE SKATE PARK. LET'S GO. QUICK!

At the skate park ...

MY BABY BURGERS - WAIT, YOU'RE NOT MY BABY BURGERS.

YOU'RE DIFFERENT.

MY DARLING CHILDREN, COME HERE! I LOVE YOUR CLOTHES ... AND YOUR HAIR.

WE FEEL DIFFERENT, DAD. IT'S THIS PLACE, YOU UNDERSTAND? SKATING HERE IS GREAT. WE FEEL ALIVE!

DARLING, DON'T OPEN A BURGER BAR HERE.

I LOVE MY BURGER BARS ...

HEFTY BURGER

BUT MY CHILDREN ARE HAPPY NOW. THEY LOVE THE SKATE PARK.

OK, I'M NOT BUYING THE SKATE PARK!

SKATEBOARDING

What do you know about skateboarding?

SKATEBOARDING THEN

1960s Skateboarding is more than 50 years old. The first 1960s skateboards are big and they aren't very fast. Today, boards are fast!

1970s

The Lords of Dogtown

The Z-Boys are a famous 1970s team of skateboarders from California. They do their skateboard stunts in empty swimming pools! Now there's a film about the Z-Boys: *The Lords of Dogtown*.

What do these words mean? You can look in a dictionary.

team   empty   film   world   air

Then and now!

SKATEBOARDING NOW

Some towns have skate parks. Skateboarders meet here and skate on ramps and pipes. Livingston Skate Park in Scotland is a very famous park. Skateboarders from all over the world go there to skate.

An Ollie

A kickflip

Skateboarding stunts have different names. The 'Ollie' and the 'kickflip' are two cool stunts.

Street skateboarders don't go to skate parks. They try their stunts on steps and walls.

Does your town have a skate park? Do you go there? Can you do any skating stunts?

Tony Hawk is a world-famous skateboarder. He can do a '900' – that's 2.5 turns in the air! There are lots of Tony Hawk PlayStation games.

Tony Hawk

Can you find these words in the pictures?
swimming pool   steps   walls

SKATE STYLE

Skateboarding is cool – the clothes, the music, the boards, and the people!

THE MUSIC

Skateboarders like different styles of music, but they never listen to quiet music! Some skaters like punk. Some skaters listen to hip hop or thrash metal or emo. (*My Chemical Romance* and *Green Day* are emo bands.) Music is very important in skating videogames, too.

THE CLOTHES

Skateboarders wear T-shirts, 'hoodies' (a top with a hood), baggy jeans and trainers. You can run and do stunts in these clothes. *Nike SB, Kr3w* and *Volcom* all make cool skating clothes. Skaters often wear 'beanies', too. These are hats - Juju wears a beanie in *Spooky Skaters*. Non-skaters also wear these clothes. They want to be cool!

Skaters call boards 'decks'.

THE BOARDS

Skateboards are all different. Most good boards cost about 70 Euros. Expensive boards are about 200 Euros. There are many different designs. Some skaters put stickers on their boards, too. Sometimes new skating trainers come with stickers.

Every year, teenagers try skateboarding for the first time – and they never want to stop! So, what do they like about skateboarding?

SKATE TALK

I always feel great after skating - I don't think about my problems! I learn new stunts at the skate park but I skate next to my house, too. I like skating in new places - it's fun. **Christopher, 15, USA**

Skating clothes are great. I have some *Alien* T-shirts and I like *Kr3w* clothes, too. My trainers are *DC* from the USA. I love beanies, too – I've got twenty! **Vincent, 13, England**

I love music and skateboarding! I'm in a rap band - hip hop music is cool. I skate and listen to music on my iPod. I can do some good stunts on the pipe! **Rachna,14, Scotland**

This is my favourite deck – it's my design. Some people hate graffiti, but I think it's cool. I want to be a designer. I design my friends' decks, too – they like my style. **Petra, 14, USA**

Look around your classroom. Are your friends wearing skate clothes? How many of them can skate? What do you think of skate style?

Find these words in the pictures.
top (hoodie)   hood
trainers   hat (beanie)
baggy jeans   graffiti

What do these words mean? You can look in a dictionary.
style   wear   design/designer   sticker   band

PAGES 6-11

Before you read
You can use a dictionary for these activities.

1 Put these words into the sentences.
secret stunts burger park
skateboard alive flip skater
a) A skate … is where people go to skate.
b) Don't tell your friends, it's a … .
c) I'm hungry. Let's have a … .
d) My friend loves skateboarding. He can do lots of good … . For example, he can do a … .
e) My new … goes really fast. It's great!
f) These animals are …, they aren't dead.
g) Look at that … on the ramp! She's doing a great stunt.

2 Match the two parts of the sentence.
a) You can go up or down
b) I've got a new board so I'm
c) This place is spooky
d) They live in a different

i) land. They don't speak English there.
ii) the new ramp. It's fun.
iii) learning to skate now.
iv) at night when it's dark.

After you read
3 Are these sentences true or false? Correct any mistakes.
a) Ben, Leila and their friends go to the skate park every morning.
b) Ben is building a ramp in the skate park.
c) Patty has got a new skateboard.
d) Roland and Patty laugh at Ben, Leila and their friends.
e) The Land of the Dead is down under the skate park.

4 Complete the sentences with the names.
Zomboy Jinx Spooky Skaters Patty Rip Roland
a) … tries to skate, but he isn't very good.
b) … and Roland are brother and sister.

c) The ... go to the skate park at night.
d) ... and Hex both like Jinx.
e) ... likes the new ramp.
f) ... teaches Juju a new stunt.

5 What do you think?
a) Are Roland and Patty happy now? Why / Why not?
b) Juju says: 'The Land of the Dead is dead boring!'
Why is it boring for the Spooky Skaters, do you think?

PAGES 12–19

Before you read
6 Choose the right word. You can use a dictionary.
a) I'm hungry. Let's go to the *skate park / burger bar*.
b) *Ghosts / Clothes* are people who aren't alive. They're dead.
c) You can do skating stunts on the ramp and the
paper / pipe.
d) Hello *darling / friendly*. How are you today?

7 Guess the answers to the questions about pages 12–19.
Then read and check.
a) Who meets the Spooky Skaters?
b) Who learns to skate?
c) Who wants to buy the skate park? Why?

After you read
8 Write these things in the correct order.
a) Patty gets some cool new clothes.
b) The Spooky Skaters want to help Roland and Patty.
c) Roland and Patty's dad talks about his idea for a
new burger bar.
d) Roland and Patty's and their mum and dad go to
the skate park.
e) Rip teaches Roland and Patty a 'Rip Flip'.
f) Roland does a stunt on the pipe.

9 What do you think?

   a) What do you think of Roland and Patty's dad's idea?

   b) Do you like Patty's new 'look'? What can Roland do to be cool?

PAGES 20-25

Before you read

10 Guess the answers to the next part of the story.
Read and check.

   a) Do Roland and Patty go back to the skate park?

   b) Does Roland and Patty's dad buy the skate park and build a burger bar?

After you read

11 Order the sentences. Who says what?

   a) 'Great hair! Don't wash it.'

   b) 'I want to learn your cool stunts.'

   c) 'Always remember your spooky skater teachers!'

   d) 'That's great skating!'

   e) 'I've got an idea.'

   f) 'We want to talk to dad about his burger bar.'

12 Complete the sentences with the names.
**Roland and Patty's mum   Roland and Patty's dad   Patty
Ben and Leila (x2)   Roland**

   a) … think Roland and Patty are good skaters.

   b) … want to learn some cool new stunts.

   c) … talks to the children's dad about the burger bar.

   d) … wants Roland and Patty to be happy and have friends.

   e) … has cool green hair.

   f) … can skate very fast.

13 What do you think?

   a) What happens to Roland and Patty next?

   b) Is it important to be cool?

   c) What can you do to make new friends?